Leah is eight years old. It is getting late, and tomorrow is Earth Day!

"Oh, mommy!" Leah says. "I can't wait!"

Leah's mom laughs. "Yes, it will be fun. We will go out and pick up trash. Then there will be a contest to see who picks up the most trash. The winner gets a green ribbon!"

Leah loves this! "Oh, mommy, I hope I win the ribbon!" She turns and hops in excitement.

"You just might," Leah's mom says. "For now, it's bedtime, though."

Leah gets in her PJ's and lays down in bed. Her mom walks in the room to say goodnight.

"Goodnight, Leah. See you in the morning," her mom says.

"Goodnight, mommy," Leah says as she yawns.

Leah's mom turns on the nightlight and quietly walks out the door.

Leah has a wonderful dream! She is at the park, and they are announcing the winner of the green ribbon. Leah had won! She screamed in delight and runs up to get the ribbon. Just then, Leah wakes up. It is Earth Day now!

She jumps out of bed and gets dressed. She runs into the kitchen where her mom was making pancakes. "Good morning, mommy! It's Earth Day!"

"Yes, it is," her mom says. "A great breakfast to start a great day, too!"

Leah hops up and down. "YUM!! I love pancakes!"

Leah's mom smiles. She sets the pancakes on the table.

When they are done eating, Leah and her mom drive to the park.

"Mommy, can I go on my own this year," Leah asks.

"I guess, but meet back here soon," her mom says.

"Yes!" Leah runs off to look for trash. There is lots of it. She finds bottles, cans, boxes, and much more. It was such a shame. All this stuff was making the world dirty. Leah picks up everything she can find and puts it in her bag.

Soon, she comes to the town's garden. She hates the sight. The pretty garden was wrecked by all the trash. She runs around the whole garden, picking up trash. She grabs bottles from the flowers. She takes plastic bags out of the trees. (If she can reach them) She even finds nasty old cans in the bushes.

The bees were really happy about this. They finally have clean flowers. They buzz all around Leah, singing a little bee song. Squirrels chatter and run in a circle. Birds fly around her and sing their song.

Leah loves this! All the animals were becoming friends with her. "Oh, you poor animals," Leah says. "You never had a clean home until now. At least, not for a long time." She decides to hop and dance along with them.

She spins, and she twirls, she hops and she swirls. She is laughing the whole time.

"I better go clean some more places," she says. "Good bye, little animals!" She runs towards the baseball fields.

This place disgusts her. Trash! Trash everywhere! There is more trash than she could imagine! She gets right to work.

When she is about halfway done cleaning the baseball fields, she stops and takes a break. She realizes it was lunchtime, so she takes her lunch out of her backpack.

Leah's lunch is a peanut butter and jelly sandwich, an apple, some potato chips, and a juice box. As she eats her sandwich, a cat comes up to her. It looks like it didn't have a home, and it probably hadn't eaten in days.

Leah breaks off a piece of her sandwich and gives it to the cat. "You poor thing," she says. "You know what, I'll name you Snowflake." Snowflake purrs at the sound of the name. Leah giggles.

Together they eat the lunch until it is all gone, then Leah gets back to work. Snowflake helps her out.

Leah even found trash hidden under the bases! She is proud of all the cleaning she is doing.

Snowflake grabs a wrapper and brings it to Leah. She takes the wrapper and puts it in her bag. "You know what, Snowflake, we make a good team," she says. Snowflake purrs.

Soon, they have the place nearly spotless. They decide to rest a bit. All the cleaning they had done really made them tired.

They lay on the grass and watched the clouds pass by. "Who knew cleaning could be so fun," Leah says. Snowflake seems to agree. She meows softly.

"I wonder if my mom would let me keep you as a pet," Leah says. "That would be cool. We could hang out with each other every day, and you could be there to meet me after school. Then we would play and all kinds of fun stuff. You know what? I'm going to take you with me so I can ask."

Leah gets to her feet and tells Snowflake to follow her. Together, they go to the city hall. This is not nearly as bad as the baseball fields, but there is still trash.

"Let's get to work, Snowflake," Leah says. Snowflake meows and starts searching. Leah runs around with her bag waving in the air. She finds a few wrappers in the city hall's flowers. She grabs all of them and puts them in her bag.

Snowflake finds paper, cans, and boxes to bring to Leah. This is not nearly as much work as the baseball fields. They are almost done.

Leah inspects behind the building while Snowflake checks the front. They each find plenty of trash.

"Great job, Snowflake! We're done!" Leah says. Snowflake jumps in the air with joy.

"Now we'll go to the creak," Leah suggests, so off they went.

The creak is awful! It is brown and dirty. Cans, bottles, all kinds of things are in it. Leah slowly creeps down into the creek. She rolls up her pants and wades in.

Snowflake doesn't want to get wet, so she just gets the trash at the edge of the creak.

Leah looks at the dirty, brown water. "We'll have to tell people that the water is so yucky, so they can clean it up. I don't know how," Leah says.

Soon, most of the creak was cleaned up. Leah grabs a few more pieces of trash and climbs out.

She sits down with Snowflake for a little to let her legs dry in the sun.

"What if Mom says no? What if I can't keep you," Leah says. This sad thought really troubles her. She thinks for a little. "If she says no, I can always come and visit you can't I?"

Snowflake meows sadly. Leah doesn't want to only be able to visit Snowflake. She wants to live with her.

Leah stood up. "I guess we'll just have to hope for the best. Come on, let's go to the park and see who wins the green ribbon."

When they get there, Leah handed her bag to the judges. Then she walks over to her mom.

"Mom, can I keep this cat? We have become really, really good friend, and I named her Snowflake."

Leah crosses her fingers as her mom thinks about it. Snowflake stands still, hoping she'll say yes. Please say yes, please say yes, Leah thinks.

Leah's mom raises her head after thinking for about a minute. Leah's hopes got really high.

"I suppose you can," her mom says.

Leah and Snowflake leap into the air. "YES!!" Leah screams.

"Oh, wait," her mom says. "They're announcing the winner." Leah freezes.

The speaker clears his throat. "We have had many people this year, and they all found lots of trash. We only have one winner, though. This year's winner of the green ribbon is…" A drum roll began. Dadadadadadadadadadachong! Leah gets really hopeful, and so does Snowflake.

"LEAH!!" the speaker shouts.

Leah leaps into the air. She grabs Snowflake and ran up to collect her ribbon. She walks up to the microphone.

"This makes me really happy that I won! I really care about the Earth, and I hope you all do, too. I couldn't have won it I didn't meet this amazing cat Snowflake." Leah picks up Snowflake and shows her to everyone.

The whole crowd begins to cheer and clap. Tears of joy run down Leah's cheeks. "Thank you!" she says. "Like I said, I really care about the Earth. I hope you all care too, that is what we are her for isn't it?"

The crowd goes wild about Leah's words, and Leah walks over to her mom, followed by Snowflake.

"I am so proud of you, Leah!" her mom says.

"Thanks, mom," Leah says happily.

Snowflake purrs and rubs herself against Leah. "I can't believe this," Leah says.

"Let's go home," her mom says. They all get in the car. Leah stares at the green ribbon the whole ride home.

The ribbon has a picture of Earth, and above the picture it says "Great Cleaner." Under the picture it says "Go Green." It just all feels like I am dreaming.

We get home and eat spaghetti for supper.

When I am done eating, I wait for Snowflake to finish, and I give her a bath. She rolls around in all the bubbles, and the mud and dirt all washes off of her fur.

Her white color really begins to show. She fits the name Snowflake really well now. She is pure white instead of a dirty, yucky brown color. Leah takes her out of the bathtub and dries her off.

Leah shows her around the house. She really likes it in her room, so Leah looks for some old pillows. She puts them in a little pile next to her bed. Next, she goes into the basement and grabs a really warm blanket that is never used. She places the blanket on top of the pillows. Now Snowflake has a nice, comfortable bed to sleep on at night, and it's right next to Leah's bed.

Leah's mom agrees that they'll go to the store in the morning to look for cat supplies.

"Hey, mom, can you hang my ribbon up in my room," Leah asks.

"Of course I can," Leah's mom says. She goes downstairs and grabs a hammer and nail. Then she goes into Leah's room and hammers the nail into the wall.

Leah hands her mom the ribbon, and she hangs it up on the nail.

The ribbon looked great with all the nature posters on Leah's wall.

"The ribbon doesn't only belong to me," Leah says.

"Who else," her mom asks.

Leah walks over to her window and opens it. The fresh breeze blows in.

"Well, it belongs to me. It belongs to Snowflake. It belongs to you. In fact, you know what? That ribbon belongs to everyone in the world who cares about nature. Not just one person is better than all others. This ribbon is a symbol of friendship. All of the people who care shall team up together and protect the world."

Leah's mom is impressed. "Those are very wise words, Leah. I am very proud of you. I can't wait until your father returns from Florida so he can hear about this. You are caring, loving, and very nice. I don't know what could make me more proud at the time."

Leah walks over and picks up Snowflake. Together, the two of them stand by the window. The cool breeze blows through their hair and fur.

Leah's mom walks over to join them. "What are you looking at," she asks. She wraps her arm around Leah.

"The nature, Mom," Leah says. "We are looking at the pretty nature.

Leah's mom smiles. The three of them all stand at Leah's window, looking at the nature.

"We could go out into the nature," Leah's mom suggests.

Leah smiles. "That sounds like a great idea. How about you get Snowflake ready, and I'll go grab my jacket."

Leah's mom starts to brush Snowflake's fur while Leah goes to the entry way.

Leah scans the hooks and finds her favorite jean jacket. She slips on the jacket and straightens it out.

"Mom! I'm ready!" Leah calls out.

Leah's mom comes down with Snowflake in her arms. Snowflake's fur has been brushed neatly. She looks really good.

Leah's mom puts on her own jacket and opens the door. Snowflake and Leah walk outside, followed by Leah's mom.

They walk around, picking up any trash they see. Soon, they come to a very pretty scene. There was a fresh creek now. Green grass grew all around, and squirrels hopped everywhere. Birds were singing in the tall trees. Leah and her mom could definitely tell that all the cleaning they had done did something.

Leah, her mom, and Snowflake all stood together in the cool breeze, looking at the wonderful nature.

www.ingramcontent.com/pod-product-compliance
Lightning Source LLC
Chambersburg PA
CBHW060023300526
45794CB00003B/1267